# Manners
# Can Be Fun

## REVISED EDITION

## BY MUNRO LEAF

J. B. LIPPINCOTT COMPANY

PHILADELPHIA AND NEW YORK

ISBN–0–397–31603–8

Library of Congress catalog card number 58-5611

Printed in the United States of America

Having good manners is really just living with other people pleasantly.

If you lived all by yourself

out on a desert island, others would not care whether you had good manners or not.

It wouldn't bother them.

But if someone else lived there with you, you would both have to learn to get along together pleasantly. If you did not, you would probably quarrel and fight

all the time

*or*——

stay apart and be lonesome

because you could not have

a good time together.

Neither would be

much fun.

Most of us don't live

stay apart and be lonesome

on desert islands

So this is

what

we

do—

# WE
# MEET PEOPLE

# HOW DO YOU DO?

If I am a boy,

when I meet you for
the first time I smile
and shake your hand.

If you are a lady

or a girl

I take my hat off.

# HOW DO YOU DO?

If I am a girl,

when I meet you for the
first time I smile and
hold out my hand to you.
I don't just stand

with my mouth open
and leave you holding
out *your* hand.

# If we already

## know you

### we say

## Good morning

### or

## Good afternoon

### or

## Good evening.

Very often the people we like
most live in the same house
with us.

We see them so often we
sometimes forget to be as
nice to them as we are to
others.

Most of the time it is just
because we do not think of it,
so let's see how we start
the day.

We get up
in
the morning

when we should

and we don't
have to be called

more than once.

We wash ourselves

and brush

our teeth

without fussing

and

making

faces.

And we don't leave our

clothes and towels around

for others to pick up.

**15**

When we are at

a good time

we eat what we

about pleasant things

the table we have

because

should and talk

we have seen and done.

# We don't have

## Puffy Cheeks

from talking with our

mouths full.

And we don't
CHOKE

because we don't drink
when we still have
food in our mouths.

Other people like to
talk to us because

 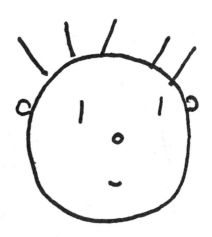

we wait until they finish
talking before we start.
We don't try to shout
louder and butt in

 like

goats.

If we want something

we

say

PLEASE

We say THANK YOU
if you help us or
give us something or
do things for us.

Before we leave the table

we ask if

we

may

be

excused.

And say 😊 THANK YOU 👋

if we are told we may.

# PLAYING

When I play
with other boys

we take turns doing the things
we want to do.

If we are playing games we
follow the rules.

One of us doesn't always
try to change things so that
he will win.

We play for fun.

When I play
with other
girls

we share our things and take turns doing what we like to most.

We don't whine and cry or quarrel when we don't have everything our way

and

go

home

angry.

There are some
people we don't
like to play with
and here they are

# THE PIGS

They have all sorts of toys
but they never let anyone else
play with them.

They just squeal
## THAT'S MINE

This is a
WHINEY

Whineys always have lumps in their throats and cry because they can't do just what they want to.

They whine if they can't have things they should not.

They whine if they can't go along when they should not

and they whine when other people tell them, No.

OH, How They Whine.

# THE NOISEYS

They shout and scream
and yell

until I can't even think.
They make so much

NOISE

they make me tired

# This is a ME FIRST

who never took turns.
He wore his arms off grabbing things
first. He wore his legs off
pushing in every place first and his
face is this way because he always
tried to see first.

# SMASH * RIP * RUIN

**SMASH** is never happy unless he is breaking things— his things—your things— everybody's things.

**RIP** is terrible. She destroys everything that she can tear. Books, dresses, paper —everything.

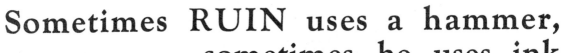

Sometimes **RUIN** uses a hammer, sometimes he uses ink or paint and sometimes he doesn't use anything but his hands. But he always spoils things so that no one can enjoy them any more.

# PUTTING THINGS BACK

SMASH, RIP and RUIN nearly always destroy the things they use.

If they don't they forget to put them back where they belong.

Then other people come along and step on them or have to put things back for them.

Don't be a
### SMASH
### RIP
### or
### RUIN.

# VISITING

When we go to
visit someone and
have a good
time

we THANK them when
we leave and say
GOODBYE.

Whether we are visiting or at home,

or at school, or at play—

if other people like to do things

with us, we probably have good manners.

NOW

let's have a look at some

creatures whose manners

are just plain painful.

You can see why

nobody would want to

have them around.

Here are two people so tiresome it's hard to tell which is worse—

BRAGGER

who tells you all the time how great he is and how he can do anything better than anybody else,

and SHOW-OFF

who is miserable if everybody isn't paying attention to her. Every minute of every day she is really saying the same thing over and over—"LOOK AT ME. LOOK AT ME. LOOK AT ME."

And here is another one who is no fun to be with—

WON'T TRY

Unless he knows he can do something best he won't play games or do anything to help others have fun.

And slumped like a lump in the corner is

SULKY

She can't have everything her own way, so she is just going to sit and sulk, hoping to make everybody else as unhappy as she is making her silly self.

This little smudge is a
WON'T WASH.
The first lesson in manners he needs is what to do with soap, water, a toothbrush and a comb, before somebody dumps him out with the trash.

And here goes a BATHROOM WRECKER, who makes a mess when he does wash. He drops clothes, wash cloths, towels anywhere. He makes puddles on the floor, leaves dirt rings in the tub and bowl, hair in the brush and comb, melts the soap, and never has put the cap back on a toothpaste tube. How would you like to live with him?

When we are old enough to go to school, most of us already know that being a MESSY DRESSER isn't how to be bright.

And let's hope we are fair enough so we don't squawk and screech answers without taking turns or raising our hands.

MANNERS at school are mostly being FAIR.

# SNOOPERS

walk
right into rooms
where other people are
when the doors are closed.

If they knocked first and asked if they might come in, people would not call them SNOOPERS.

This is **TOUCHEY.**

Wherever he goes he touches things. He never thinks whether he should or not— Maybe it's because he hasn't any head—he is all hands.

And Touchey has a cousin named GRABBER who always takes the biggest and the best piece of anything.

Some people don't know it but there are

## TELEVISION MANNERS

too. Pigging the best seat and always saying what shows to look at is being crude and rude. And if you don't stop watch-ing TV when you are told to—well, we don't have to tell you what kind of manners those are— Do we?

See if you can't use a Radio or Record Player at the right time and place, so you don't make other people unhappy with too much NOISE.

# MOUTH MANNERS

Some tiny babies don't know that they shouldn't suck their thumbs. But these creatures—

YAWNER

SNEEZER

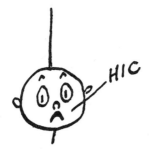

COUGHER

BURPER

HICCUPPER

are old enough to know they should cover their mouths and say EXCUSE ME!

# Here you see a car full of bad manners.

Old Grumpy with his arms folded and that sour look on his face is making everybody with him unhappy. Ever since they started he has kept on whining, "When are we going to get there?" and "How much farther is it?"

His trash-tossing sister is trying to make our whole country as much of a mess as she is herself.

And here all by their selfish selves are two of the meanest mannered creatures we ever met.

When their parents go out and have to leave them behind, they raise an awful fuss. They are unfair and nasty to anybody who comes to take care of them.

Wouldn't you think that just once they would say to their parents, "Have a good time," then behave themselves so that nobody had to worry about them at all?

# WHEN
# NIGHT
# COMES

It is time for sleep

and people who
like us all
the day

Say GOODNIGHT.

Then it is time

for us

to

go.

 Only WHINEYS

stand about

while we

are first

in—

# BED

•

Be kind to

ANIMALS.

They have feelings, too.